Luna's
Stellar Sound Search

To my amazing children, whose boundless imaginations and fearless spirits inspire me every day. Your creativity and ability to be unapologetically yourselves are a constant reminder to dream without limits.

First, she landed on a moon
made of marshmallows.
"Mmm, marshmallow moon!"
she mumbled.

Luna used her telescope
to spot tiny twinkling stars.
"Twinkle, twinkle little stars!" she teased.

Next, Luna pounced onto a purple planet full of playful penguins. "Penguins on a planet? Perfect!" she pondered.

Suddenly, a big blue blast-off shook the stars.
"Blast-off!" shouted Luna, holding onto her helmet.

Luna saw a dancing drone flying by.
"A daring drone in deep space!" she declared.

"This galaxy is gigantic!" she gasped.

Finally, Luna watched a
fiery fireball streak across the sky.
"What a fantastic fireball!" she exclaimed.

Author

Jessica is mom of four, a wife, and a former elementary school teacher with a passion for making learning fun and engaging. Originally from Ohio, she grew up surrounded by creativity and a love for teaching. When she's not writing, you'll find her cooking up family favorites, exploring the outdoors, or diving into hand-on projects with her kids. Her experiences as a teacher and a mom inspire her to create resources that bring joy and connection to families everywhere.

www.ingramcontent.com/pod-product-compliance
Lightning Source LLC
Chambersburg PA
CBHW070343120526
44590CB00017B/2993